Jill

Hello Baby!
Kathleen Petruch
I St

Kathleen Petrich

Illustrations by T. Thomas Seelig

Book Publishers Network
P. O. Box 2256
Bothell, WA 98041
425-483-3040
www.bookpublishersnetwork.com

Copyright 2015 Teaspoon Books, LLC
Illustrations by T. Thomas Seelig

10 9 8 7 6 5 4 3 2 1

ISBN   978-1-940598-79-6
LCCN 2015946831

Dedicated to our parents who taught us
to love dogs, Seattle, and each other—and not
necessarily in that order.

Acknowledgment and thanks go to the
special dogs and humans in our lives.

Hello, baby! We look forward to meeting you soon. Our world has so many exciting places for you to see with us …

In the winter, we will go to the Seattle Aquarium and see clownfish and other brightly colored sea creatures.

At the waterfront, we'll ride the Seattle Great Wheel,
go waaaay up high, and won't be scared at all!

To celebrate the Chinese New Year, we'll go to the International District and see the Dragon Gate.

In the spring,
we will visit Pike
Place Market.

There, we'll see fish fly… with a little help from the fishmongers.

Boats, bikers,
and dogs—we'll
watch them all
at Green Lake.

At the Seattle
Art Museum,
we'll see a man
who never stops
working—the
Hammering Man.

In Fremont, we'll explore under the Aurora Bridge. Maybe we'll find a monster troll with his "toy" car.

In the summer, we will wander around Woodland Park Zoo and check out the giraffes.

We'll board a ferry and ride across Puget Sound.

And we promise you won't get seasick.

We will see the Space Needle.

On a beautiful summer day, we will picnic at
Mt. Rainier National Park.

We'll visit the Market Theater Gum Wall in Post Alley. Some of us might even add to the display.

We will look for orca whales in Puget Sound and maybe see one breach!

Pirates will march before us at the Seafair Torchlight Parade, but we'll keep you safe from those scallywags.

We'll look up, up, up in August—and follow the Blue Angels doing their tricks in the air during Seafair.

When it's hot, we
will travel to the
Cascade Mountains
and keep cool.

In the fall, we will stroll around the Seattle Art Museum's Olympic Sculpture Park and look at the large outdoor art.

During Labor Day Weekend, we'll listen to all sorts of music at Bumbershoot.

While the weather is still good, we'll take a break at an outdoor café and maybe have a bite to eat or something special to drink.

When the holidays arrive, we'll ride the carousel at Westlake Mall and go round and round but never get dizzy.

And we'll go to a performance of the Pacific Northwest Ballet's Nutcracker.

After twelve months of exploring, we'll celebrate the new year by watching fireworks blast off from the Space Needle.

Now, it's time for rest.

About the Illustrator and Author

Illustrator **T. Thomas Seelig** demonstrated her artistic skills as a little girl and continues to create works of art. She purposely drew the illustrations in this book out of perspective to show children that it is okay to break art's adult-mandated rules. Yes, coloring can go outside the boundary lines. A business owner, Seelig lives in Olympia, Washington, with her husband and two dogs.

Author **Kathleen Petrich** is an attorney who lives in Seattle, Washington, with her husband and Jill, a Bernese mountain dog, the inspiration for the drawings in this book.